better
together*

*** This book is best read together, grownup and kid.**

a
kids
book
about

a kids book about

ICE CREAM

by Kim and Tyler Malek
Founders of SALT & STRAW®

A Kids Book About
Editor Emma Wolf
Head of Design Rick DeLucco
Publisher Jelani Memory

DK
Senior Production Editor Jennifer Murray
Senior Production Controller Louise Minihane
Managing Editor Hazel Eriksson
Publishing Director Mark Searle

This American Edition, 2026
Published in the United States by DK Publishing,
a Division of Penguin Random House LLC
1745 Broadway, 20th Floor, New York, NY 10019

First published in Great Britain in 2026 by
Dorling Kindersley Limited, 20 Vauxhall Bridge Road, London SW1V 2SA
A Penguin Random House Company

The authorised representative in the EEA is
Dorling Kindersley Verlag GmbH. Arnulfstr. 124, 80636 Munich, Germany

A CIP catalogue record for this book is available from the British Library

ISBN 978-0-2417-7661-2

DK books are available at special discounts when purchased in bulk for
sales promotions, premiums, fund-raising, or educational use. For details, contact:
DK Publishing Special Markets, 1745 Broadway, 20th Floor, New York, NY 10019, or
SpecialSales@dk.com

Printed and bound in China

Photography by Stephanie Shih

www.dk.com

akidsco.com

For Susannah Kelly.

Susannah was one of the first people
to believe in our dream—and one of
the very first Salt & Straw scoopers.

She believed deeply in creativity and
community, and helped shape Portland's
art scene by bringing people together. Her
spirit lives on in all she helped create, and
in all of us who carry her light forward.

Intro
for grownups

You probably picked up this book because you like ice cream. (Excellent choice.) But if you stick with us for a few pages, you'll see that this book isn't *really* about ice cream. Or at least—not *only* about ice cream.

Ice cream has a funny way of waking something up in us. A sense of curiosity. A sense of wonder. It slows us down. It gets us off our phones. It gives us a reason to sit next to someone we love and just...be there.

Over the years, we've watched kids feel braver, grownups feel lighter, and entire families share moments they didn't know they needed—all because of a scoop of something cold and sweet. This book is an invitation to explore curiosity, creativity, and connection with your kid. To try things that might not work. To talk about how things feel. To make something together—whether it's a flavor, a memory, or a moment.

So read this book together. Ask questions. Make a mess. And don't worry about doing it "right." Ice cream doesn't have rules.

And neither does wonder.

There's only one rule for ice cream.

It's the only food in the world with...

NO RULES!

WELL, ACTUALLY, IT SHOULD PROBABLY BE FROZEN. (BUT EVEN IF IT DOES MELT, YOU'VE NOW GOT A VERY TASTY SOUP, RIGHT?)

Ice cream is surprisingly
easy to make!

YOU CAN MASH, SQUEEZE, STEEP, STIR, SWIRL, TWEEZE, OR LAYER ANY FLAVOR YOU WANT. REALLY!

Did you know we once made ice cream out of spicy chips, and even Dungeness crab?

That doesn't mean they
tasted good, but we tried!

AND IT WAS
STILL ICE CREAM.

Maybe you're wondering if this book is about how to make ice cream.

It definitely is, and yet...

IT'S ABOUT SO

MUCH MORE.

My job is to make ice cream and come up with new flavors every day.

My job is to create ice cream shops—those places you go to get your ice cream.

Together, we've made and sold

2,000 FL

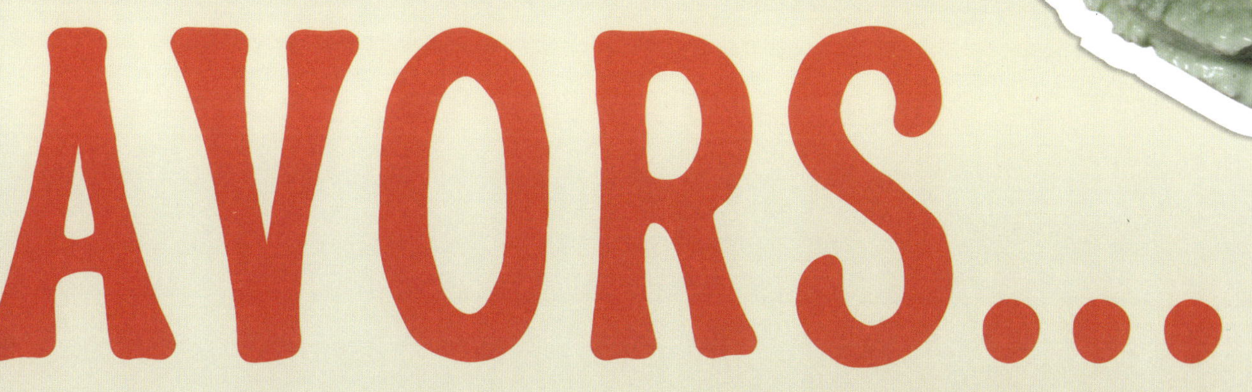
AVORS...
and tested over 10,000 FAILURES.

Ice cream isn't just ice cream.

It sparks...

FUN,
EXPERIENCES,
FREEDOM,
CREATIVITY,
ADVENTURE,
A REASON TO HANG OUT,
HOPE,
CONTENTMENT,
BELIEF,
NEW IDEAS,
AND A THOUSAND
MORE THINGS.

To put it simply,

ICE CREAM SPARKS

WON

DER!

WE'VE MET KIDS WHO HAVE
OVERCOME FEARS—WITH A
LITTLE HELP FROM ICE CREAM.

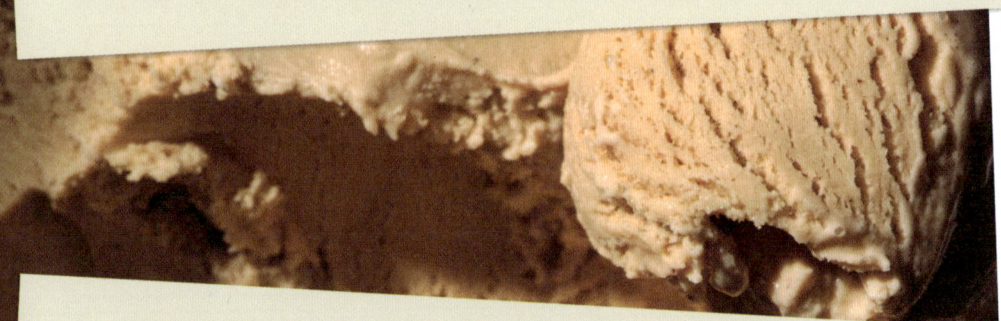

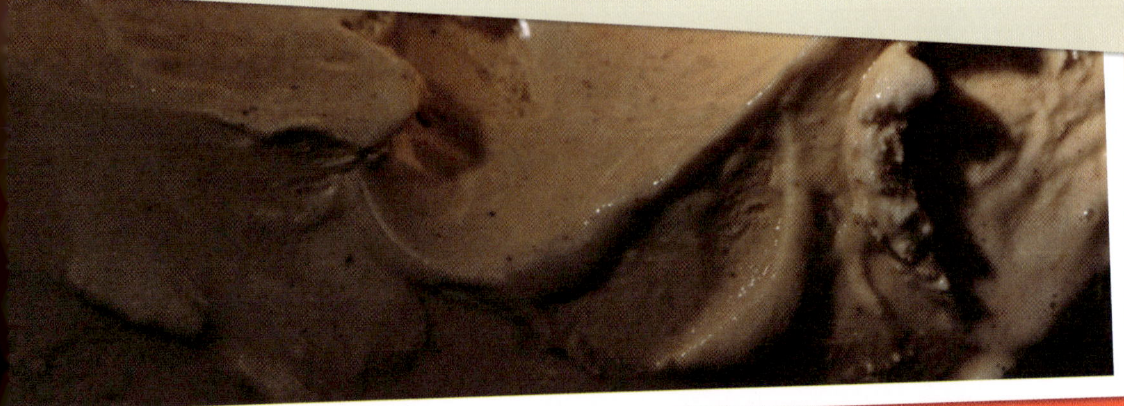
WE'VE SEEN GROWNUPS CRY
WHILE ENJOYING A SPECIAL
MOMENT WITH A LOVED ONE—
ALL WHILE EATING ICE CREAM.

WE'VE WITNESSED COUNTLESS SMILES, TEARS, HUGS, AND LAUGHS IN OUR ICE CREAM SHOPS OVER THE YEARS.

BECAUSE GOING TO GET ICE CREAM ISN'T JUST ABOUT "GOING TO GET ICE CREAM."

When you eat ice cream, it's hard
to be on your phone, because
your ice cream might melt.

That means you're fully present...

WHICH IS
AWESOME!

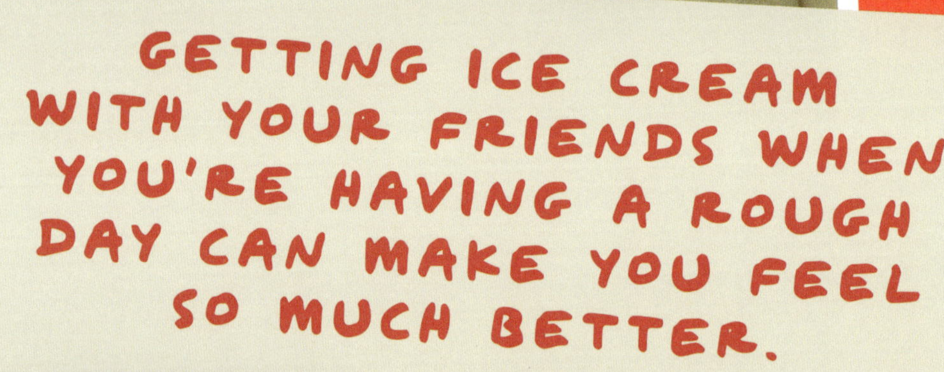

GETTING ICE CREAM
WITH YOUR FRIENDS WHEN
YOU'RE HAVING A ROUGH
DAY CAN MAKE YOU FEEL
SO MUCH BETTER.

Not just because of the cream
and sugar, but because of the

FRIENDS.

This is why I wanted to start my first ice cream shop all the way back in 1996.

I BELIEVED IT
COULD BE A WAY
TO BRING
PEOPLE
TOGETHER,
TREAT
EMPLOYEES
REALLY WELL,
AND SPARK
AMAZING
MOMENTS!

But the closer
I got, the more
scared I felt.

I didn't
want to fail.

But like with any new ice cream flavor, sometimes, you just have to give it a try!

Eventually I found the courage...

AND SOME HELP FROM MY COUSIN TYLER!

I took all of my money
and opened our first scoop shop.

And people showed up...

AND
THEY
JUST
KEPT
COMING!

So many magical
moments were created.

All made possible by freezing
some milk and sugar.

But how does it all work?

Well, let me tell you!

Every ice cream flavor
starts with a question:

HOW DO YOU WANT
SOMEONE TO FEEL AS THEY
EAT YOUR ICE CREAM?

THINK ABOUT FLAVOR:
WHAT WILL IT TASTE LIKE?

AND TEXTURE:
WHAT WILL IT FEEL LIKE
IN SOMEONE'S MOUTH?

AND TEMPERATURE:
HOW COLD ARE WE
TALKING HERE?

THERE ARE [THREE] MAIN COMPONENTS TO EVERY ICE CREAM.

The base, which is the foundation to all your flavors. My favorite is a simple pinch of salt with either vanilla or chocolate, but you can get as creative as you'd like, ranging from honey lavender to black pepper and olive oil.

The mix-ins, which means any chunks you want to fold into your flavor. I love using my favorite candies or baked goods. These will be your main source of texture—do you want chewy brownies, crunchy nuts, or decadent cookies?

And the variegates, which is a technical term for "sauces." These sauces are typically the quickest to melt on your taste buds and offer the first punch of flavor. I love using local berry jams, rich fudge sauce, and, of course, our famous homemade caramel.

And here's what makes
ice cream so amazing:

YOU CAN START WITH ANY OF THESE PIECES.

For example, one of our most
famous ice creams is called

CREEPY CRAWLY CRITTERS.

We use real edible bugs

which are grown in San Francisco
by one of the first edible bug
farmers in the country.

So, believe us when we say that ice
cream can be made with anything!

ALL IT TAKES IS AN IDEA.

So...

WHAT WOULD YOU MAKE ICE CREAM OUT OF, IF YOU COULD PICK ANYTHING IN THE WORLD?

HOW DO YOU WANT YOUR ICE CREAM TO MAKE PEOPLE FEEL?

WHAT DO YOU WANT IT TO TASTE LIKE? LOOK LIKE?

Every person has their
own creative style.

When you create an ice cream
flavor, it could take the form of:

A BEAUTIFUL DRAWING,

A WATERCOLOR PAINTING,

A POEM (WE'VE HEARD A LOT OF THESE BEFORE!),

OR A BUSINESS PLAN FOR MAKING YOUR OWN ICE CREAM SUCCESSFUL!

THERE'S NO LIMIT TO WHAT YOU CAN MAKE.

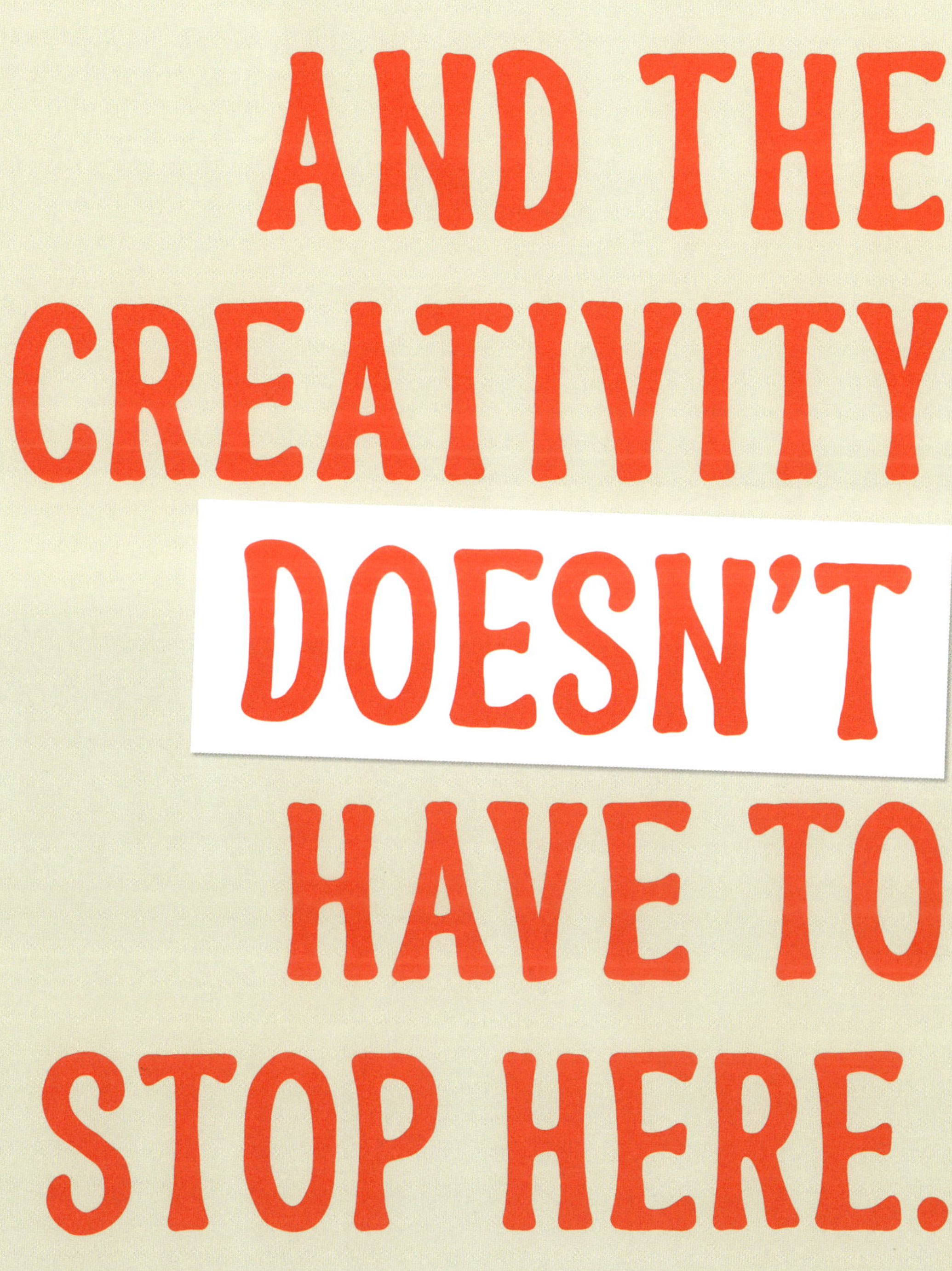

AND THE
CREATIVITY
DOESN'T
HAVE TO
STOP HERE.

We hope you take
the wonder and joy
of ice cream into

EVERY PART

OF YOUR LIFE!

YOUR OWN RECIPE:

1 ½	cups heavy cream
1	cup chocolate syrup
½	cups sweetened condensed milk
½	cup water
½	cup (your favorite) crumbled cookies

· ·

Stir together the cream, sweetened condensed milk, chocolate syrup, and water. Pour the ice cream mix into an ice cream maker and churn until it reaches a soft serve texture, about 20-25 minutes. Stir the cookies in while the ice cream is still soft. Eat immediately or store in your freezer.

Outro
for grownups

If you've made it this far, chances are your kid has ideas. Big ones. Weird ones. Possibly ones involving bugs, or candy, or both. That's kind of the point.

Ice cream teaches us something simple but important: you don't have to know the ending before you begin. You just have to start—with curiosity, care, and a willingness to try.

So keep the conversations going. Ask your kid what they'd make. What they'd change. How they want people to feel.

You don't need special tools or perfect answers. Just time, attention, and a little bravery.

We hope this book reminds you that creativity isn't rare—and joy isn't complicated.

Sometimes, it's just milk, sugar, and showing up for each other.

Pretty cool, right?

About The Authors

Kim and Tyler Malek combined their love of ice cream and creating special moments to found Salt & Straw, a beloved scoop shop that now boasts 40 locations across the country.

Kim and Tyler prioritize delicious ice cream flavor combinations alongside local community engagement and support of nonprofit organizations. Over the years, they've supported equal rights through Basic Rights Oregon and The Trevor Project, food waste and insecurity with Urban Gleaners and Share Our Strength, child cancer research through Alex's Lemonade Stand Foundation, and the preservation of our protected landscape through the National Park Foundation.

Using ice cream as a blank slate for storytelling, Kim and Tyler fearlessly explore ingredients, discover emerging artisans, and share inspiring, unifying experiences through their business.

 @saltandstraw    www.saltandstraw.com

Made to empower.

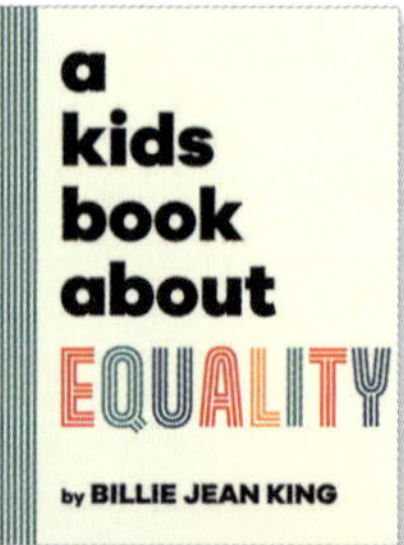

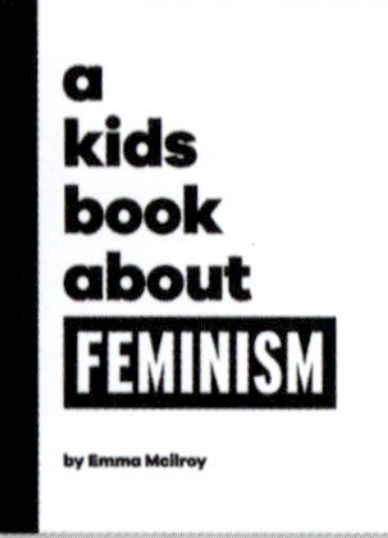

Discover more at akidsco.com